Ways into Science

# Changing Materials

Written by Peter Riley

**W**
FRANKLIN WATTS
LONDON • SYDNEY

First published in 2001 by Franklin Watts
96 Leonard Street, London  EC2A 4XD

Franklin Watts Australia
56 O'Riordan Street
Alexandria, NSW 2015

Series editor: Rachel Cooke
Assistant editor: Adrian Cole
Series design: Jason Anscomb
Design: Michael Leaman Design Partnership
Photography: Ray Moller (unless
otherwise credited)

A CIP catalogue record for this book
is available from the British Library

ISBN 0 7496 3959 8

Dewey Classification 536

Printed in Malaysia

Picture credits:
Pictor International p. 22b

Thanks to our models:
Jordan Conn, Nicola Freeman,
Charley Gibbens, Alex Jordan,
Eddie Lengthorn and Rachael Moodley

# Contents

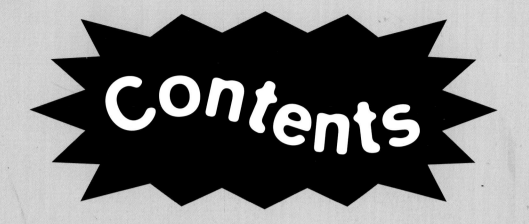

# Different materials

Everything is made of materials.

wool

wood

wax

Materials can change in many different ways.

sand

dough

clay

Some materials, such as clay, can be changed into different shapes.

Some materials change when they are wet.

When dry sand gets wet, the sand grains stick together.

Some materials change when they get hot.

When a candle burns, the heat melts some of the wax.

Can you think of other ways materials change? What are they?

# Changing **shape**

You can change the shape of some materials by stretching them.

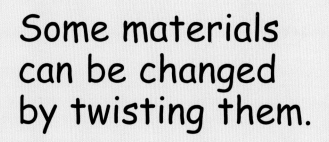

A balloon stretches when you blow it up.

Some materials can be changed by twisting them.

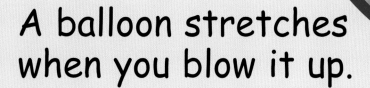

String can be twisted together.

Look closely at the string. How has it been made?

You can change the shape of a material by bending it.

A plastic straw can be bent.

You can squash some materials too.

An empty cardboard drinks carton can be squashed.

Try changing the shape of a sponge in these four different ways. What happens when you let go?

Daniel is pulling on both ends of the modelling dough.

As he pulls, the dough stretches.

This head-band stretches to keep Lucy's hair in place.

10

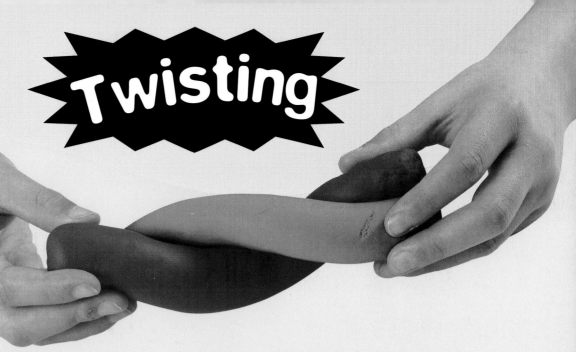

# Twisting

Daniel turns the ends of two pieces of dough in opposite directions. This makes the dough twist.

This pasta has been twisted into spirals.

What is Daniel doing to the dough now? Turn the page to find out.

# Bend it! Squash it!

Daniel is bending the dough! Lots of materials can be bent.

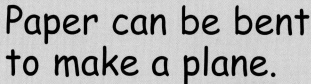

Paper can be bent to make a plane.

Now Daniel pushes down on the dough. It is squashed flat.

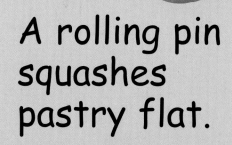

A rolling pin squashes pastry flat.

Collect some different materials together. Find out how many ways they can change by stretching, twisting, bending and squashing them.

| | Bend | Squash | Stretch | Twist |
|---|---|---|---|---|
| rubber band | ✓ | ✓ | ✓ | ✓ |
| plastic ruler | ✓ | | | |
| paper bag | ✓ | ✓ | | ✓ |
| metal drinks can | ✓ | ✓ | | |
| woolly sock | ✓ | ✓ | ✓ | ✓ |

Record your results on a table.

Toby is making a model out of clay.

He changes the clay by pulling and squashing it.

An adult puts the clay model in a very hot oven. The heat in the oven makes the clay change.

The clay is baked hard. It cannot be pulled or squashed.

But the clay can be changed in a different way.

Now if Toby drops his model it will break into small pieces.

This is bread dough. What happens when it is baked?

Think about your answer then turn the page.

# Cooking **food**

The dough makes bread.

It is hard on the outside but soft in the middle.

Food changes when it is heated. It is cooked.

Bacon is cooked in a frying pan.

Slices of bread are heated in a toaster.

The heat permanently changes the bacon. The bacon was soft. Now it is hard and crispy.

The bread is permanently changed, too. Now it is hard and brown.

Lucy spreads butter on her hot toast. What happens to the butter? Turn the page to find out.

# Melting materials

The butter melts.

Try this test to find out more about melting.

metal fork

plastic beaker

unlit candle

Leave these objects in a sunny place for three hours. The objects are heated by the Sun.

bar of chocolate

ice cubes

The metal fork and plastic beaker become warm.

The wax candle goes soft.

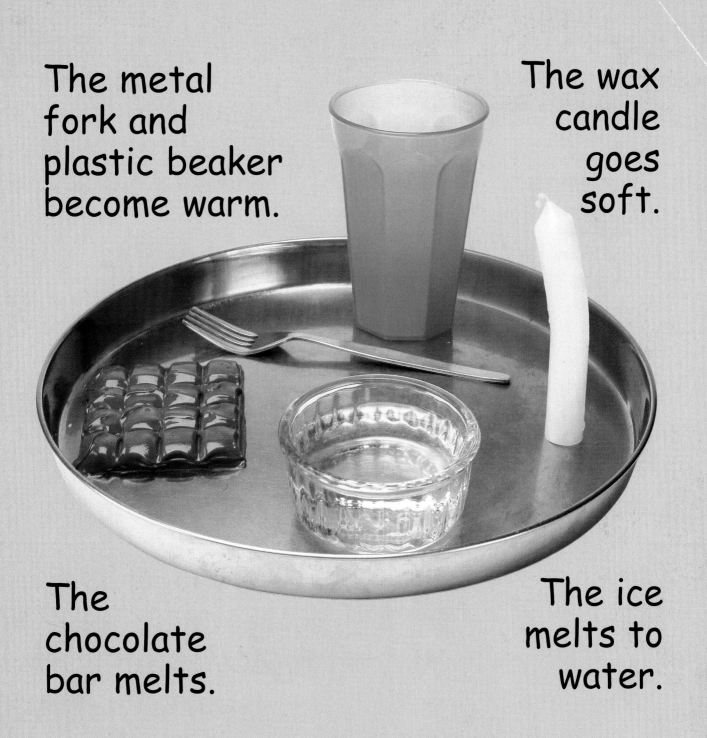

The chocolate bar melts.

The ice melts to water.

What happens if the water is put in the cold freezer again?
Turn the page to find out.

# Freezing liquids

The water freezes to solid ice again!

Water, orange juice and tomato sauce are liquids. When you pour them they flow.

Pour some water, orange juice and tomato sauce into an ice tray.

Put the tray in a cold freezer.

Take the tray out a few hours later.

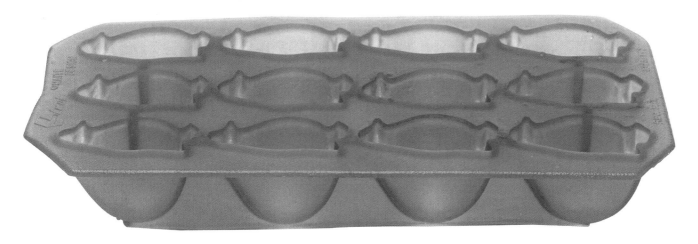

The water, orange juice and
tomato sauce are all hard.
None of them flow.
They have changed
from liquids
to solids.

How could the
solids be
changed back
to liquids?

Water can be changed by cooling and heating.

When water becomes very cold it freezes – the water turns to ice.

In very cold weather, dripping water freezes into icicles.

When water becomes very hot, it boils. You can see bubbles in boiling water.

The boiling water turns into very hot steam. Steam is a kind of gas.

Steam has made this mirror misty.

Draw a picture with your finger in the mist. Your finger gets wet.

The steam has turned back into water.

# Dissolving materials

When sugar mixes with a hot liquid it disappears. This change is called dissolving.

Some materials like instant coffee colour the water as they dissolve.

If a material does not disappear in water, it does not dissolve.

Try this test.

Nadia pours warm water into six jars.

She stirs bath salts, instant coffee, flour, oil, sugar and sand into different jars.

What do you think happens? Turn the page to find out.

Nadia looks at each material in the water.

The bath salts, instant coffee and sugar have dissolved.

She finds that sand, oil and flour do not dissolve.

# Nadia makes a record of her results on a table like this one.

| Material | Dissolved | Didn't dissolve | Other change |
|---|---|---|---|
| instant coffee | ✓ | | Turned water brown |
| bath salts | ✓ | | Turned water blue |
| sand | | ✓ | Grains sunk to bottom of jar |
| sugar | ✓ | | No other change |
| oil | | ✓ | Floated on surface |
| flour | | ✓ | Went very lumpy |

Do any other materials disappear completely like sugar?
How can you tell there is sugar in the water?

# Useful words

**cook** - to prepare food for eating by heating it in some way.

**dissolve** - to mix a solid into a liquid so that it seems to disappear and become part of the liquid.

**freeze** - to change from a liquid to a solid. Water freezes into ice when it gets cold.

**gas** – the air around us is a kind of gas, so is steam. A gas does not have a shape and is often invisible.

**ice** - water that has been frozen solid.

**liquid** - a material that is runny and has no shape of its own, such as oil or water.

**materials** - what things are made of.

**melt** – to change from a solid to a liquid. Ice melts into water when it gets warmer.

**permanently** - when something is changed and cannot be changed back to how it was.

**solid** - a material that has its own shape and is not runny.

**steam** - when water is heated and boils, the liquid turns to a gas called steam.

# Some answers

Here are some answers to the questions we have asked in this book. Don't worry if you had some different answers to ours; you may be right, too. Talk through your answers with other people and see if you can explain why they are right.

**page 7**     The rest of the book will answer this question. Simply, you can change a material by changing its shape, mixing it with something else or heating or cooling it (that is, taking heat away). Sometimes heating something will make it melt, sometimes it will make it burn.

**page 8**     The string has been made of several thin strands of thread twisted together. Look at woollen, cotton and silk thread as well and see how they are made.

**page 9**     When you stretch, twist, bend or squash the sponge and then let go, it will spring back to its normal shape. Can you think of other materials that do this as well?

**page 21**     You could change the solids back to liquids by heating them. This will happen naturally if you leave them out of the freezer, but you could speed it up by putting them in a sunny place. Don't forget to put them on a plate! See what happens to them: do they all melt at the same time? Which takes the most time to become a liquid again? Keep a record of your results.

**page 27**     The coffee and bath salts disappeared but they coloured the water so you could tell they were there. Table salt also dissolves like sugar. Test the water for sugar by tasting it – remember to wash your hands first.

# Index

## About this book

**Ways into Science** is designed to encourage children to begin to think about their everyday world in a scientific way, examining cause and effect through close observation, recording their results and discussing what they have seen. Here are some pointers to gain the maximum use from **Changing Materials**.

• Working through this book will introduce the basic concepts of changing materials and also some of the language structures and vocabulary associated with it (for example melting, cooking and comparatives such as solid and liquid). This will prepare the child for more formal work later in the school curriculum.

• On pages 11, 15, 17, 19 and 25 children are invited to predict the results of a particular action. Ensure you discuss the reason for any answer they give in some depth before turning over the page. In most cases there is only one accurate answer, but don't worry if they get it wrong. Discuss the reasons for the answer they gave then create other scenarios and get the children to predict the results again.

• Follow the tests in this book but also encourage children to draw on their everyday experiences too, particularly with food. For example with melting butter (page 17-18), ask when will the butter melt faster? Will it always melt? What else happens to the butter, does it change colour?

• Relate the discussions about changing a material's shape (pages 8-12) to using forces (pushing and pulling).

• Link the way the materials change (or do not change) to the process of selecting appropriate materials for a particular purpose. For example, on page 10, would a head-band made of material that does not stretch be as useful? Or, on page 19, would a metal fork be useful if it melted in the Sun?